Mother Teresa

Caring For All God's Children

by Betsy Lee
Illustrated by Robert Kilbride

DILLON PRESS, INC. MINNEAPOLIS, MINNESOTA

Library of Congress Cataloging in Publication Data

Lee, Betsy, 1949-
    Mother Teresa: Caring for all God's children

    (Taking part; 12)
    SUMMARY: A biography of the nun whose many years of
working with poor and outcast people has been recognized with
the 1979 Nobel Peace Prize.
1. Teresa, Mother, 1910-   —Juvenile literature.
2. Nuns—India—Biography—Juvenile literature.
3. Missionaries of Charity—Juvenile literature. [1. Teresa
Mother, 1910-   2. Nuns] I. Kilbride, Robert. II. Title.
BX4406.5.Z8L43   266′.2′0924 [B] [92]   80-20286

ISBN 0-87518-205-4

Dillon Press, Inc., 500 South Third Street
Minneapolis, Minnesota 55415

Printed in the United States of America

MOTHER TERESA

Mother Teresa is known around the world for the Missionaries of Charity, an order of hardworking nuns and brothers. The Missionaries of Charity serve the poorest of the poor in five continents. Mother Teresa has received many awards for her work, most recently the 1979 Nobel Peace Prize. She has been honored by popes and prime ministers.

Born in Skopje, Yugoslavia, Mother Teresa left home at eighteen to join the Loreto nuns in India. For many years she taught at Saint Mary's High School in Calcutta and served as the school principal. One day she heard God's call—a call to leave the school and to serve the poor while living among them. Mother Teresa helped the abandoned and starving people who lived and died on the streets of Calcutta.

Her work was the beginning of the order that became part of the Catholic church in 1950. Women from all over India and from foreign countries came to join Mother Teresa. She started homes for the dying, abandoned children, lepers, and retarded people. For Mother Teresa no one is too poor or outcast to receive God's love. She sees her work as God's work—caring for all God's children.

Agnes woke up early on Easter morning. She put on her best dress. Her brother and sister put on their good clothes, too. It was a special day, and they were all excited.

Agnes lived in Skopje, Yugoslavia, where she was born on August 27, 1910. Her full name was Agnes Gonxha Bojaxhiu. The Bojaxhius were very religious people. Easter was an important time for them.

In Yugoslavia Easter was the greatest holiday of the year. Everyone went to church early in the morning before the sun rose.

Agnes's mother told the children to hurry. They did not want to be late. Agnes and her family walked down the dark streets to the Catholic church. A large crowd was gathered there.

One by one, the people entered the church. It was dark and full of mystery. The only lights that Agnes could see were three tall candles. They stood on a table in the middle of the church. This was the holy table. A beautiful cloth lay on the holy table. The people believed that the cloth was the body of Jesus Christ. Agnes kissed the cloth. Her family and friends did, too.

Then they stood and waited. Suddenly the priests appeared, and the people began to sing for joy. Each person held a lighted candle. The whole church was filled with light.

The priests lifted up the beautiful cloth that lay on the holy table. Holding the cloth high, they

walked out of the church. All the people followed. They sang songs and walked around the church three times.

What a beautiful sight! Hundreds of candles flickered in the darkness. The priests' robes were bright with gold thread and jewels that shone in the moonlight.

The priests marched back into the church with the people behind them. The service went on until sunrise. When it was over, everyone stepped out into the early morning sunshine. They shouted, *"Hristos vaskrese!"* Christ is risen!

Now Easter had really begun. It was the beginning of a new day. It was the beginning of spring. And for many it was the beginning of a deeper religious faith. To them Christ was the light of the world. His love made the darkness go away. That was something to shout about.

Agnes believed this with all her heart. On this Easter Sunday she was very happy. The love of Christ was real to her. She enjoyed going to church. At school she liked to listen to the priests talk about Jesus. They said that Jesus loved little children and the sick and the poor. Agnes wanted to live like Jesus when she grew up.

When she was twelve, Agnes decided to become a missionary. Missionaries travel to foreign lands to tell people about God's love. Agnes knew it was not enough to talk about God's love. She also wanted to show it by loving others.

She heard about a group called the Loreto nuns. They worked in India. There were people in India who did not know about God's love. They were very poor. Nobody seemed to care about them. Agnes decided to become a Loreto nun and help these people.

It was not an easy decision. She would have to leave Yugoslavia and live in India. India was thousands of miles away, far from her family and friends. Agnes came from a happy family. She loved her parents and her brother and sister. She did not want to say good-bye.

At eighteen Agnes did leave Yugoslavia and join the Loreto nuns. First she had to go to Ireland where she learned to speak English. That was the language the nuns spoke. After a year of training, Agnes was sent to India.

For two years she lived in Darjeeling in northern India. She went there for more training. Darjeeling was very beautiful. The tall mountains surrounding the city reminded her of her own home in Yugoslavia.

Then she was sent to teach at Saint Mary's High School in Calcutta. The school was run by Loreto nuns. They lived in a convent on the school grounds. The students lived with the nuns and went to school there. Agnes taught geography and history. She enjoyed teaching.

In 1936 she took her final vows as a nun. She had to promise three things: to love God with all her heart, to live a simple life, and to obey God. When Agnes became a nun, she took a new name. She chose the name Teresa, meaning "the little one."

Sister Teresa was the smallest nun in the convent. She was only five feet tall. There was nothing special about the way she looked. But when she smiled, a light shown from her eyes. She had an inner joy and beauty.

The little nun was very popular with her students and the other teachers. They liked to be near her. Her smile made them happy. She taught at Saint Mary's for seventeen years. For several years she was the school principal. She came to be known as Mother Teresa.

Mother Teresa was not completely happy at Saint Mary's. Something was wrong. A concrete wall surrounded the convent and high school.

Inside the wall, the students laughed and played. They did not have a care in the world. The school grounds were covered with green grass and palm trees. It was a quiet, peaceful place.

Outside the wall, the people were very poor. They lived in a terrible slum. It was a crowded, noisy place. The children were naked and dirty. They slept in the streets under cardboard boxes and burlap bags. They ate scraps of food from garbage cans. Many of them died because they did not have enough to eat.

Mother Teresa could see these poor and suffering people from her bedroom window. It saddened her. How could she help them? She asked God to show her what to do.

One day God told her. Mother Teresa was riding on a train to Darjeeling when she heard God's call. "The message," she said, "was quite clear: I was to leave the convent and help the poor while living among them. It was an order. I knew where I belonged, but I did not know how to get there."

When she was a girl, God had told Mother Teresa to leave her homeland to become a nun. Now she would have to become a new kind of nun. "It was the most difficult thing I have ever done," she remembers. It was even harder than leaving her family and her country.

At first the Catholic church did not like Mother Teresa's idea. Nuns were not allowed to live outside the convent walls. Her decision had to be approved by the archbishop of Calcutta. Then the pope in Rome had to give his approval.

Finally, on August 16, 1948, Mother Teresa was allowed to leave the convent and live among the poor. When she walked out of the convent, the door closed behind her. She found herself on a Calcutta street, alone, in the dark. She had no money, no place to sleep, no friends. But she knew that God had a special job for her to do. He would provide what she needed.

First she spent three months at Patna Holy Family Hospital learning the skills of nursing. She needed medical training to care for the sick. Mother Denegal, an Austrian nun, was head of the hospital. Mother Teresa told Mother Denegal about her plans to live among the poor. The sisters who joined her would live that way, too.

"We shall eat rice and salt," said Mother Teresa.

Mother Denegal was shocked. "You will all die," she said. "Your nuns must keep strong and well to do God's work."

This was good advice. Mother Teresa changed her plans. She and her nuns would eat enough to stay healthy. But they would eat simple food.

When Mother Teresa returned to Calcutta, she needed a place to live. Father Henry was a priest and her good friend. He went to see a man named Michael Gnomes. "Could you find some place for Mother Teresa to stay?" asked Father Henry. "A mud house or a hut will do."

Michael Gnomes had an eight-year-old daughter. She heard what Father Henry said. "Daddy, the rooms upstairs are empty," she reminded her father. "Mother could come here."

"Yes," said Michael Gnomes. "Send her here."

Father Henry shook his head. "This is too good for her. She wants something simple."

But Michael Gnomes said she must come. "She is a nun. She must be treated well. She does the work of God."

Early in 1949, Mother Teresa moved into the second floor of Michael Gnomes's house. She brought a suitcase and a chair. That was all she had. Michael let her stay in his house for free.

Mother Teresa's first job was to start a school. She found a mud hut in the slums for her schoolhouse. She had no table, no chairs, no blackboard, and no chalk. Still, the children came.

On the first day Mother Teresa taught them the alphabet. She drew the letters with a stick in the mud. She taught the children to wash and comb their hair. She taught them to pray. And she told them that God loved them.

Mother Teresa no longer dressed like a nun. Like other Indian women, she wore a plain white wraparound *sari*. And, like the poor, she begged for her food. In every way she wanted to be like the poor people she served. Each morning Mother Teresa woke up early. She prayed that God would give her strength for the day. Then she went out into the slums, bringing medicine to the sick and teaching the little children.

It was hard work to do alone. One night there was a knock at her door. Mother Teresa opened the door. She was surprised to see a young woman standing before her. Mother Teresa knew the woman from Saint Mary's High School. She had been one of her students.

"Mother, I have to come to join you," said the young woman.

"It will be a hard life. Are you prepared for it?"

"I know it will be hard," she answered. "I am prepared for it."

That night Mother Teresa thanked God for sending her first helper. The woman took Mother Teresa's first name, Agnes. Sister Agnes and Mother Teresa became close friends.

News of Mother Teresa's work spread. One by one, more young women came to join her. Next came Sisters Gertrude, Dorothy, Margaret, and Mary. They all wanted to help serve the poor.

Soon there were twelve nuns. Jesus also had twelve helpers when he began to serve the poor.

Like Jesus, Mother Teresa taught the sisters to serve God by serving others. And she showed them how to serve by doing it herself.

Mother Teresa told her nuns that they must put their love into action. They must nurse the sick, feed the hungry, and comfort the lonely. All these things should be done with a happy smile. "In the slums we are the light of God's kindness to the poor," she told them. "Let no one ever come to you without leaving better and happier."

The sisters worked hard. They got up at 4:30 in the morning. Together they prayed and worshiped God. Then they ate their breakfast. At 8:00 they went to tend the sick and poor.

Before long the poor people came to know what Mother Teresa's nuns looked like. The nuns wore white *saris* with a blue border, just like Mother Teresa. When the people saw them coming, they smiled. The children sang for joy.

The sisters came home for lunch. Then they prayed. In the afternoon there was more work to be done. But the sisters did not spend all their time working. At night they played hopscotch and tug-of-war. They were like a big happy family. After playing, it was time for prayer again. Then there was complete silence. The sisters fell fast asleep.

Mother Teresa did not go to sleep. She stayed up late at night to write letters to young girls who wanted to join her. She also wrote thank you letters to people who sent her money for carrying on the work. And she spent many hours writing the constitution.

The constitution said what Mother Teresa and her nuns believed. In it were the rules that they followed. "We are called the Missionaries of Charity," wrote Mother Teresa. "A Missionary of Charity must be a missionary of love. She must be full of love in her own soul and spread that same love to the souls of others."

Like other nuns, Mother Teresa's nuns made three promises. But they also took a fourth vow. They promised to serve only the poor. They did not accept money for their work. It was a free service to those who needed it.

In 1950 Mother Teresa and her nuns became an official part of the Catholic church. This gave great happiness to the little nun and her team of young helpers. Mother Teresa became a citizen of India in that same year.

Young women from all over India and many foreign countries came to Calcutta. They wanted to work with Mother Teresa. Soon there were too many nuns to live in Michael Gnomes's house. The sisters were sleeping side by side like sardines.

Each night they prayed for a house of their own.

At last an offer came. Father Henry took Mother Teresa to see the house. It had three stories, and there were other buildings, too. They were built around a large courtyard.

"Father, it is too big," said Mother Teresa. "What will we do with all that room?"

Father Henry smiled. "Mother, you will need it all. There will be a day when you will ask where to put all your people."

Mother Teresa did not have the money to buy such a big house. The archbishop of Calcutta heard about the good work that Mother Teresa was doing. He wanted the good work to go on. He gave her the money to buy the house.

The new house was located on a street called Lower Circular Road. Mother Teresa and her nuns still live there today. It is in the center of Calcutta. While the nuns are praying, they can hear the sounds of the city. Buses zoom by, dogs bark, and wooden carts go clackety-clack.

Calcutta is a crowded city. It has been called a "nightmare city." More than seven million people live there. Many of them do not have houses. They sleep in the alleyways and on sidewalks. Their clothes are cotton rags. When they get sick, they cannot afford to go to the doctor. And it seems as if nobody cares when they die.

One day Mother Teresa found an old woman lying on the sidewalk. She was nearly dead. Rats and cockroaches were crawling over her. Mother Teresa took the woman to a hospital. The hospital would not let the woman in because she had no money. Mother Teresa stayed with her while she died in the street.

"Cats and dogs are treated better than this," said Mother Teresa. She decided that there should

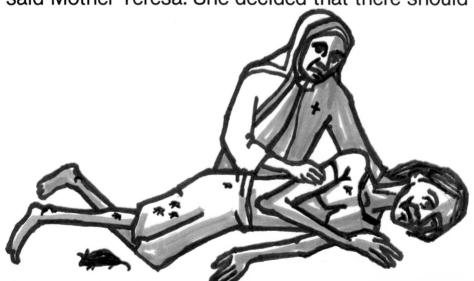

be a place where people could die in comfort. They should not pay any money to go there.

Mother Teresa marched to the Calcutta city hall. She talked to the police chief. "It is a shame for people to die on our city roads," she told him. She asked him to give her a place where she could take care of the dying. "Give me at least a room," she begged.

"Yes, there is a place," said the police chief. He was glad to have someone take care of the dying. The city had a bad name because it could not care for all the poor people.

There was an empty rest house near the Temple of Kali. Kali is the Hindu goddess of death. Most Indians believe in the many gods of the Hindu religion. Mother Teresa told the police chief that the rest house was just what she had in mind. She knew that many Hindus came to the temple to die.

Mother Teresa named the house Nirmal Hriday, "The Place of Pure Light." Poor people could go there to die in peace. "We want to make them feel that they are wanted and loved, that they are somebody special," she said. Each person was treated with kindness. Many of them got well because of the good care they received.

Still, some people were not pleased with Mother Teresa's work. There were Hindus who did not like a Christian woman working on the temple grounds. They became very angry. Sometimes they threw stones at Mother Teresa and her nuns.

The police chief came to see what was the matter. He saw the nuns working. The sisters washed the sores of the sick and put bandages on their wounds. They fed the hungry. All this they did with great love.

The police chief was amazed. He told the Hindus, "I promised I would get that woman out of here. And I shall. But first you must get your mothers and sisters to do the work these nuns are doing. In the temple you have a goddess of stone. Here you have a living goddess."

The Hindus kept throwing stones at the nuns. One day a crowd gathered outside the temple. A Hindu priest lay dying on the sidewalk. No one would help him. Mother Teresa picked him up and took him to her Home for the Dying. She cared for him herself. The priest died smiling. After that there was no more trouble from the Hindus.

Mother Teresa did not care if someone was a Christian or a Hindu, rich or poor. She loved all people the same. "They are all children of God," she would say.

On the streets of Calcutta there were many children who needed love and care. Little babies were thrown away like trash in garbage cans. Their parents could not afford to keep them. Some children were crippled. Many were sick.

Mother Teresa decided to open a house just for children. It was called the Children's Home. She told the people of Calcutta that she would take care of all unwanted babies. Hundreds of them came. The police brought little children. The hospitals sent newborn babies. No child would ever be turned away, said Mother Teresa.

The Children's Home is filled with laughter. The nuns enjoy working there. Often the children climb into their arms and ask for a piggyback ride. They like to be swung in the air. "Look at them," says Mother Teresa, "they are hungry for love."

People from around the world write to Mother Teresa asking for a child. Some married couples have no children. They are happy to adopt a boy or girl from India. Mother Teresa has a big picture album of her children. In it there are pictures of children wearing American cowboy hats. Some are sledding in Switzerland. Others are horseback riding in England. All of them are smiling and proud beside their new parents.

The Children's Home and the Home for the Dying are just two of Mother Teresa's projects.

Over the years there have been many more. She started workshops for men out of jobs. She gave free food to the starving. And she opened clinics for the sick, especially those who suffer from leprosy. Leprosy is a terrible disease that causes ugly sores on the body. Those who have this disease are called lepers. Lepers are outcasts in India.

When Pope Paul VI came to India in 1964, he heard about Mother Teresa's leprosy work in Calcutta. The United States had given him a fancy white car to ride in on his trip. He gave the car to Mother Teresa. She sold it for thousands of dollars. With the money she built a place to live just for lepers. They could go there for treatment.

More and more people began to hear about Mother Teresa's good works. She was asked to start schools and homes for children in many parts of India. The government gave her a free pass on the Indian railroads. Using the pass, she could visit her homes in different cities.

The prime minister of India, Mr. Nehru, invited Mother Teresa to open a children's home in New Delhi. New Delhi is the capital city of India. It was a great honor to start work there.

Mr. Nehru attended the opening of the children's home. "Sir, shall I tell you about our work?" asked Mother Teresa.

"No, Mother," said Mr. Nehru. "You need not tell me about your work. I know about it. That is why I have come."

Political and religious leaders all over the world heard about Mother Teresa. The pope asked her to come to Rome to open a center for her sisters. She started homes in South America, Africa, and the Middle East. "Wherever there are poor," said Mother Teresa, "we shall go and serve them."

Mother Teresa's work grew and grew. She needed more help. In 1963 she started the Missionary Brothers of Charity. The brothers are a group of men who work side by side the sisters in the slums.

An Englishwoman, Ann Blaike, heard about Mother Teresa's work when she was living in Calcutta. She wanted to help, too. She gathered a group of women together to raise money for Mother Teresa's projects.

The time came for Ann Blaike to go home to England. When she returned, she wanted to keep on helping Mother Teresa. In England she organized a group of women called co-workers. The co-workers helped Mother Teresa in their own country. They made bandages for the sick and sent old clothes to India for the poor.

Once Mother Teresa came to England. She saw poor people who suffered in the cities there. She told Ann Blaike that the English co-workers should help people living in their own neighborhoods. Now the co-workers help old people, crippled children, and the poor.

Many people write to Mother Teresa asking how they can help. She tells them to start a group of co-workers. In 1969 the International Association of Co-workers of Mother Teresa was founded. There are groups in Poland, in Japan, and in the far north within the Arctic Circle. The co-workers help people in their own countries and pray for Mother Teresa's work in India.

In 1950 Mother Teresa had 12 nuns to start the work in India. Today there are 1,800 nuns, 275 brothers, and 120,000 co-workers. They serve the poor, the sick, and the dying in 60 countries. Together they have helped millions of people.

Mother Teresa has become the most famous Catholic nun in the world. She has appeared on television and radio. In 1975 her picture was on the cover of *Time* magazine.

As more people hear about her, they want to support her work. She never asks for money or help. Still, the money comes. She uses it to build more hospitals and more homes for the dying and for children without parents.

Mother Teresa has won many awards for her service to the poor. In 1971 she was given the Pope John XXIII Peace Prize. This prize is the highest award in the Catholic church. That same year she won the John F. Kennedy International Award and the Good Samaritan Award in Boston.

World leaders have invited her to special ceremonies in her honor. She has dined with

presidents and princes. Always she wears her plain white *sari* and leather sandals. On her left shoulder is a cross.

In 1979 Mother Teresa won the most famous award of all—the Nobel Peace Prize. She was 69 years old. Mother Teresa's picture was on the front page of Calcutta's largest newspaper. The headline read: "The Mother of Bengal Is Now the Mother of the World."

Mother Teresa flew to Oslo, Norway, to accept the award. She received $193,000. The money, she said, would be used to build new homes for the poor. There was also to be a dinner in her honor, costing $7,000. She asked that the dinner be canceled. Instead, she wanted that money to be used for the poor, too.

The people of Norway wanted to give Mother Teresa an award of their own. They collected $60,000 and called their gift the "people's peace prize." Mother Teresa led a parade through the streets of Oslo to receive her award. It was December. There was snow, and the weather was very cold. Mother Teresa wore just her sandals and a threadbare coat over her white *sari*.

As she passed by, thousands of people cheered and waved. The parade took place at night. Everyone carried a lighted torch. Hundreds of flaming torches blazed against the dark sky.

Mother Teresa remembered marching in another nighttime parade many years ago in Yugoslavia. It was Easter Sunday. She was a little

girl. She carried a candle and followed the Catholic priests into church. They were honoring Christ, the light of the world.

Now she was at the head of the parade. Now she was honoring Christ as the priests had done so many years ago. As a little girl, she had dreamed of doing something beautiful for God. She had wanted to live like Jesus and share God's love with everyone. She had made her dream come true.

The next day, Mother Teresa received the Nobel Peace Prize at Oslo University. The people cheered her. She did not give a long speech.

These were her words. "I am very happy to receive it," she told the crowd. "In the name of the hungry, of the homeless, of the crippled, for all those people who feel unwanted and unloved—the throwaways of society. In their name I accept the award."

Many people call Mother Teresa a living saint. And yet, Mother Teresa says that she is no different from anyone else. The work is God's work, not hers. "I am a little pencil in God's hand," she says. "God is writing his love letter to the world in this way, through works of love."

The Author
Betsy Lee is a free-lance writer and photographer whose illustrated articles have appeared in the *New York Times,* the *Saint Louis Post-Dispatch,* and several magazines. She is the author of *Charles Eastman* in the Story of an American Indian series, also published by Dillon Press.

Ms. Lee received a B.A. in English literature from the University of Wyoming. She spent five years in England and now lives in Minneapolis with her husband and daughter.

The Illustrator
Robert Kilbride has illustrated several books, and his paintings are in the permanent collections of the Walker Art Center, the Minneapolis Institute of Art, and the University Gallery of the University of Minnesota. He also taught art at the University of Minnesota, the Walker Art Center, and the Minneapolis School of Art.

Mr. Kilbride was graduated from the Minneapolis School of Art and studied at the Acadèmie de la Grande Chaumière in Paris. His works have been widely exhibited in the United States and France.